FRACTALS
The Art of Math

By Anastasia Suen

CELEBRATION PRESS

Pearson Learning Group

Contents

Patterns in Nature

Stars appear as dots in clusters and in lines in the night sky. Water flows in wavy lines. Raindrops form circles when they land in a pool. Leaves grow in groups of three and four. Everywhere you look, you can find patterns in nature.

People have always enjoyed reproducing nature's patterns in paintings, drawings, and carvings. More recently, artists have used computers to create patterns. Some of the most complex and beautiful of these computer patterns are called **fractals**. Fractal patterns are made with a math **equation** that the computer uses to create regular and irregular shapes. These shapes are repeated over and over again on a smaller and smaller **scale**. The resulting pattern can look like a snowflake, a shell, a lightning bolt, the ragged edge of a coastline, or the branches of a tree.

Fractals weren't given a name until the Computer Age, but that doesn't mean they were just invented. Their origins lie in the history of math, all the way back to patterns ancient people painted on cave walls. These patterns also include the patterns from nature that ancient people carved onto rocks. Because we find this art on rocks, we call it rock art.

PACIFIC
OCEAN

UNITED
STATES

IRELAND

ATLANTIC
OCEAN

NICARAGUA

Rock Art
Around the
World

There are two types of rock art. Petroglyphs are carved into the rocks. Pictographs are painted on top of the rocks. In some places, these two types of art appear together.

Rock art has been found on every continent except Antarctica. Most of the rock art that has survived are petroglyphs. To cut patterns into the rock, ancient people used sharp stones, much as sculptors use hammers and chisels today. Since the patterns were cut into the rock, they did not disappear as the top layers of the rock wore away over time.

Most pictographs, on the other hand, have been worn away by the wind and the rain. Pictographs have only survived where the rocks are not exposed

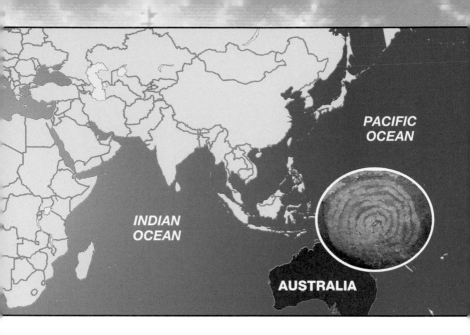

PACIFIC OCEAN

INDIAN OCEAN

AUSTRALIA

to the weather. This is why so many Stone Age paintings are found inside of caves.

Rock artists around the world recorded the world as they saw it thousands of years ago. Although these ancient artists could not have met, their art uses many of the same patterns because their **inspiration** was the same. They all marveled at the patterns in nature. This is why rock art found in different places around the world is often surprisingly similar.

Some scientists think that the circles or spirals seen in rock art were also a way to keep track of the Sun's position. They see rock art as a kind of calendar that used the Sun to count the days. At certain times, such as the summer solstice when the Sun is at its highest point overhead, sunlight shines directly on these rock patterns.

If this solar calendar theory is true, then one pattern in nature was used to count another. The patterns seen in the natural world were carved in the rock to help count the cycle of the seasons and the days of the year. Counting things, such as days and objects, led people to develop numbers and then math. Counting was a way for people to organize the world around them.

Counting Leads to Math

In the ancient world, when people hunted for their food or gathered it from the plants that grew wild, they didn't need to count very high. After all, how many buffalo could one person eat? They didn't need large numbers when they lived day to day.

To count smaller numbers, people used their bodies. With fingers and toes, people could count from 1 to 5, 10, 15, and 20. As a young child, you probably used your fingers to count or to tell how old you were.

As farming developed, people needed to use larger numbers. How many sheep did they own? How many jars of oil did they have? They needed more than ten fingers and ten toes to count their wealth. So people began keeping track of how much they owned by using a counter or token, which was a mark or an object of some kind. Each token stood for one item, whether it was a sheep or a jar of oil. Each kind of item also had a different type of token.

As cities formed over time, the need grew for better counting methods. People who lived in cities began to pay **taxes,** just as people do today. In those days, people didn't pay taxes with money. They paid taxes by bringing some of their work, such as a part of their

Sumerian clay tablet shows a tally of sheep and goats.

crops or a number of animals from their herds, to the government tax collector.

In ancient Sumeria, the city workers developed a new way to count so they could keep a record of taxes paid. They didn't use tokens or simple tally marks. They created a counting system that used **symbols** to represent groups of numbers. Different types of symbols were used to count everything, including animals, jars, and bundles of wheat.

First, the Sumerian tax collectors counted by ones, making a mark like a small cone. To count by tens, they made a small circular impression for each ten. Then the Sumerians jumped to sixty, a number they called "the big one." The Sumerians drew a 60 with a big mark.

In Egypt, the taxes paid to the pharaoh, or ruler, were based in part on how much land a person owned. This meant that the land had to be measured. Measuring space is not the same as counting sheep! Here too, the math started with the body. The land was measured by comparing it with measurements from the body. For the Egyptians, the basic measure was called a cubit. A cubit was measured from the tip of an elbow to the tip of the fingers. They also used the foot, which was the length of a person's foot, and the hand, which was the width of a person's hand. Today, people still measure the height of a horse by hands. Paces, or long steps, were also used to measure distances.

You can see why these measures needed to be standardized, which means to set as a single measure, rather than vary from person to person. The amount of tax owed could change depending on the body size of the tax collector!

To more accurately measure land, the Egyptians created a new type of math that developed into geometry, which is the mathematics of shapes. The word *geometry* means "to measure the earth." This new math also helped them to build the great pyramids.

Geometry became more scientific through the work of a Greek named Pythagoras. In his travels through Egypt, Pythagoras saw how the Egyptians used math to measure and build. After returning to southern Italy, he started a school to study math ideas in arithmetic, music, geometry, and astronomy.

Arithmetic uses numbers to add, subtract, multiply, and divide. Music is based on numbers, too. How long each musical note is heard can be counted; so can how quickly the music plays. Even which notes are played together can be calculated mathematically. The Greeks said that arithmetic was "numbers at rest" and that music was "numbers in motion." Astronomy, which studies the stars, was also "in motion." Geometry was "magnitudes at rest."

As the Greeks discussed their ideas about math, geometry began to change. Unlike the shapes in nature, which are irregular and change with time, the shapes in Greek geometry used straight lines and never changed. By experimenting, the Greeks discovered that some shapes fit together perfectly without any gaps. Today we describe this perfect fit as **tessellation**. The word *tessellation* comes from the word *tessera*, which is a small, colored tile used to make mosaics, or designs on walls and floors.

Once these geometric patterns were discovered, people used them in creating mosaic designs throughout the ancient world. You can still see these patterns today. For example, a pattern using octagons and squares is often used on floors. A soccer ball forms a tessellation with pentagons and hexagons.

The patterns formed by the tiles in this coal cover form tessallations.

The Greeks talked about points and lines. They studied shapes like circles, triangles, and squares. As they continued to study and work with geometric shapes, they developed rules to describe and measure these shapes. A Greek by the name of Euclid wrote down the rules. Today, the geometry that students study in school is called Euclidean geometry.

The work the Greeks did in geometry, along with ideas about numbers that were developed in India and Arabia, led to new and wonderful discoveries. People could use numerals to describe and record the world around them. This ability led to the invention of machines that could make things and eventually to the most amazing machine of all—the computer.

Math + Art = Computers

An idea from India helped pave the way for machines that eventually became the first computers. Computers work by using a code made of ones and zeros. Early counting systems, however, did not have a symbol for zero. If there was nothing to count, there was no need to write a number!

In India, mathematicians refined their decimal system based on tens, hundreds, and thousands by using nine numerals that are the same as we use today—1, 2, 3, 4, 5, 6, 7, 8, 9—plus 0. Their name for zero was *sunya*, which means "nothingness."

The Indian ideas spread to Arab mathematicians. They brought the nine Indian numerals to Europe by the end of the twelfth century. The Europeans called

0	1	2	3	4	5	6	7	8	9
Indian 700 A.D.									
·	1	2	3	4	5	6	7	8	9
Arabic 1100 A.D.									
0	1	2	3	4	5	6	7	8	9
Modern Arabic Numerals									

The symbols we use to write numerals have changed over time.

them Arabic numerals since they had learned about them from the Arabs.

The Arabs also brought the numeral zero from India. In Europe, the idea of having a numeral that stood for nothing was quite controversial. It was not until a mathematician named Leonardo of Pisa, or Fibonacci (1175–1250), wrote about the zero in his book *Liber Abaci* (*Book of the Abacus*) that it was accepted as a numeral.

Patterns also played a part in the development of the first computers, starting with weavers. Until the late 1700s, most people used looms to make cloth by hand. The warp threads that go from top to bottom in the cloth are attached to the loom. The weft threads that go across from side to side are added by the weaver using a tool called a **shuttle**.

The Industrial Revolution changed this age-old method when machines were built to make cloth. A mechanical loom could weave faster than a person and could easily make cloth that was all one color. Cloth with a pattern was more difficult. To make a cloth that had a pattern, the weaver had to change the weft threads. Weavers who worked on hand looms had always done this, but doing it with a machine was a challenge. How would the machine know it needed 3 inches of red thread and then 4 inches of blue in the middle of a yellow row?

A weaver works on a Jacquard hand loom in Japan.

In 1801, a Frenchman named Joseph-Marie Jacquard found a way to create patterns in silk on his mechanical weaving looms. He punched holes in pasteboard cards to create a program for the loom. The cards told the loom when to add the different colored threads. The shuttles holding the colored threads would only pass through where there was a hole punched in the card.

Jacquard's punched cards soon spread to other types of weaving. By about 1825, they were introduced in the United States. By the mid-1800s, Jacquard's power looms were making carpets in Philadelphia, Pennsylvania.

Jacquard's punched-card ideas later inspired a teacher named Herman Hollerith to create a machine that solved a large problem the United States government had. Before computers were invented to handle **calculations** with large numbers, people had to count things by hand. One large group of numbers that required a great deal of time to count was the census. In the United States, the population is counted every ten years. As the country grew, this job became more and more difficult. At the end of the 1800s, counters were still making tally marks on rolls of paper, then adding the marks together. This process was time-consuming. The government was afraid the counters would be unable to finish the 1890 census before it was time to count people all over again in 1900.

The solution came in 1890 from Hollerith in response to a competition the government held for solutions to the census problem. Hollerith won the competition by creating an automatic machine using punch cards. The cards contained information about people that the government wanted counted in the census, such as age and number of children. The census takers punched out information that applied to a specific person. Hollerith's machine read and sorted the cards.

The machine was so successful that it was used to process census information from countries around the world. In 1924, Hollerith formed a company he later named International Business Machines, which later became known as IBM.

IBM became famous as a company that made computers. Early computer programs were written on punch cards and fed into the computer, like the punch cards used with Jacquard's looms. Where there was a hole, a switch turned on. Where there was no hole, a switch turned off. This "on-off" method came from George Boole, a mathematician who created a new type of algebra in 1854. In Boole's view, the answer to complex problems was either true or false. Boole assigned a number to each of these choices. True was a 1 and false was a 0. In modern computers, Boolean algebra runs computer programs with a basic code of 1s and 0s.

The first computers were used only for math to help government and businesses work with large numbers. Their main purpose was to save time counting and calculating math problems. Then, in the 1960s, a research mathematician who worked at IBM discovered that computers could do something else—create art.

The Discovery of Fractals

In the 1960s, Benoit Mandelbrot, an IBM research mathematician, created a new kind of geometry that could be used to describe the natural world. Most people at the time thought that the irregular shapes in nature were random and chaotic, which means that they did not appear to have any order. As Mandelbrot described, "Clouds are not spheres, mountains are not cones, coastlines are not circles, and bark is not smooth, nor does lightning travel in a straight line."

A simple question aided Mandelbrot in discovering that nature's irregular shapes actually followed a pattern when looked at in smaller elements. Because these patterns repeated, Mandelbrot was able to use math to describe them.

The question, "How long is the coastline of Britain?" was asked

Benoit Mandelbrot in front of a Mandelbrot Set fractal

A closeup drawing of Cape Cod shows the longest coastline.

by Lewis Fry Richardson as he worked on measuring coastlines. The answer he came up with was "It depends." How long the coastline was depended on which tool was used to measure it.

Mandelbrot found that if you measure a coastline in yards, you get one answer. If you measure it again with feet, your answer will be a larger number that would equal more yards than the first answer.

How can the length of a coastline change? When you measure a straight line in yards, feet, or inches. the length does not change. The inches equal the same number of feet and the feet equal the yards. However, when you measure irregular edges like a coastline, the measurement *does* change, depending on what you use to measure. Why? The smaller the tool, such as a 12-inch ruler or a 6-inch ruler versus a

yardstick, the more irregular edges you are able to measure. When you measure the tiny twists and turns in a coastline, you get a bigger answer than if you bypass these edges with a longer straight line.

Look at the three drawings of a coastline above. Each drawing shows the same place with different scales. The drawing on the left shows the view that is farthest away, the drawing in the middle is closer, and the drawing on the right is the closest view. Try tracing the outline of each coastline with thread. Then measure the amount of thread you used for each drawing on a ruler, a yardstick, or a tape measure. To help you with measuring the maps, make a copy of the pages on a photocopy machine. Then tape your thread along the turns of each coastline.

Based on his observations, Mandelbrot wrote a

computer **graphic** program that repeated the same math equation over and over again. With this program, the computer created pictures of patterns that looked like natural objects. The equation became known as the Mandelbrot Set.

Mandelbrot called his new math fractal geometry. He invented the word *fractal* from the Latin word *fractus*, which means "to break." He used the word to describe a geometry that works with broken, bent, and uneven shapes. He later wrote a book called *The Fractal Geometry of Nature* that changed how many scientists viewed the natural world.

Making Fractals

Coastlines are fractals because the twists and turns of the land form patterns. In all fractals, the same pattern repeats itself on a smaller and smaller scale. Because fractals have the same pattern over and over again, they are self-similar. This means that the repeated pattern is similar to itself.

In nature, fractals are usually **random**. Random patterns are not the same on all sides. Waves crash onto rocks, so the rocks on the coastline wear away on one side. Wind from the sea blows hard against a tree, so the tree branches grow away from the wind. The rocks and the trees form patterns, but these patterns are not **regular**.

The patterns in regular fractals are repeated equally on all sides. When fractals repeat the same shape, mathematicians say that they **iterate**. To make a fractal, you repeat, or iterate, the first shape.

You can make regular, or geometric, fractals with graph paper and a pencil. A popular repeating pattern is Sierpinski's triangle, named after Polish mathematician Waclaw Sierpinski who created the pattern with triangles. To make Sierpinski's triangle, you draw smaller triangles inside of a larger one.

How to Make Sierpinski's Triangle

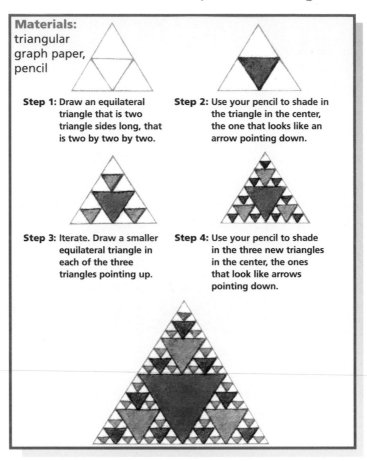

Materials: triangular graph paper, pencil

Step 1: Draw an equilateral triangle that is two triangle sides long, that is two by two by two.

Step 2: Use your pencil to shade in the triangle in the center, the one that looks like an arrow pointing down.

Step 3: Iterate. Draw a smaller equilateral triangle in each of the three triangles pointing up.

Step 4: Use your pencil to shade in the three new triangles in the center, the ones that look like arrows pointing down.

To make Sierpinski's triangle, you repeated the pattern of the fractal on a smaller scale inside the original pattern. Another fractal created by Sierpinski is called a carpet. It can also be made by repeating the pattern inside of the original shape, which is a square.

To make Sierpinski's carpet, you need to think in threes in order to have enough room for iteration. Three squares in a row gives you a middle square. Finding the middle is the key.

How to Make Sierpinski's Carpet

Materials: square graph paper, pencil

Step 1: Draw a square that is 27 squares long on each side.

Step 2: Divide your carpet into thirds. Make 9 squares that are 9 by 9.

Step 3: Use your pencil to shade in a square in the center third. This makes the center square look like a picture in a frame.

Step 4: Iterate. Divide each of the squares in the picture frame into thirds to create another picture frame in each square. Now you have squares that are 3 by 3.

Step 5:
Use your pencil to shade in the center square in each of the new picture frame squares.

You can continue to divide each of the new picture frame squares into thirds to make even smaller picture frames. At this point, you will be using the smallest squares on your graph paper, so your squares are 1 by 1.

Both of Sierpinski's fractal patterns move inside the original shape when they iterate. Another fractal pattern, named after Swedish mathematician Helge von Koch, adds on to the original shape and moves out.

Koch's fractal begins with the Koch curve. Strangely enough, the Koch curve is made from straight lines! The curve begins with a single line, which Koch called the initiator, or starter. The line is then divided into thirds. Once again, this creates a middle, so there is somewhere to repeat the pattern.

The line is flat, so Koch couldn't go inside it. Koch began to iterate by adding an **equilateral** triangle to the line in the center third. Then, Koch erased the base of the triangle so the line now had four segments. The

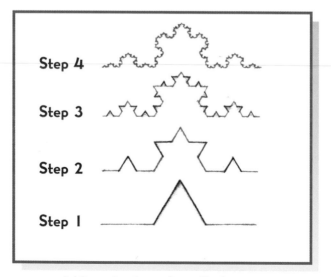

Adding triangles makes a Koch curve.

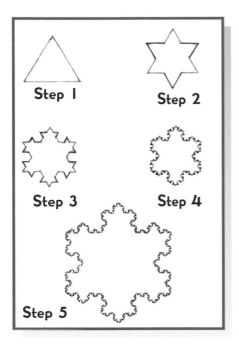

Step 1

Step 2

Step 3

Step 4

Step 5

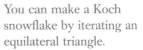

You can make a Koch snowflake by iterating an equilateral triangle.

outer thirds of the initiator line made up two segments. The two sides of the triangle that had not been erased made up the other two. This new figure was called the generator because it created something new.

Koch then repeated the generator pattern. To iterate, he divided each of the four line segments into thirds. He added an equilateral triangle in the center third, and then erased the triangle's base. Rather than moving inward, the Koch curve keeps moving outward. With four segments in the generator, each iteration increases the number of segments by four.

Fractals Inside and Out

Fractals can be used to describe and model all kinds of things. Scientists have used fractals to model how the planets move, how plants grow, the flow of music, and weather patterns.

Fractals have even helped to solve problems. Engineers have always had trouble with antennas, such as those built into cellular phones. Long, thin, straight wires do not make the best antennas. Engineers have discovered that fractals can help. More wire can fit into a smaller space if it is bent into the shape of the Koch curve. The shape also improves the antenna's operation.

Computers have helped scientists use fractals in practical ways. Other machinery have also shown fractals in places no one had thought to look. As cameras became more complex, scientists were able to use them to take photographs inside the body. After years of looking at patterns on the outside, scientists discovered that humans had fractals on the inside! From head to toes, the human body is filled with fractals.

How you breathe is a perfect example of a fractal. When you breathe, air goes down your windpipe.

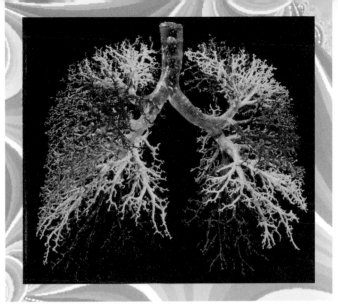

The branching of the bronchi in the human lungs form fractals.

Your windpipe, or trachea, is a single tube. Like a fractal, the trachea splits in two when it reaches the bronchial tubes. One tube goes to the left lung and one goes to the right. Inside each lung, your bronchi split into smaller tubes, which split again and again and again, until the air you breathe reaches the smallest tubes, your bronchioles. The tubes in your lungs iterate as they split in two again and again and again. Just like other fractals found in nature, your lungs are irregular. Your right lung is slightly larger than your left lung.

Your lungs aren't the only fractals in your body. Your blood vessels also iterate as they travel through your body. Your brain folds again and again, just like

Fractal Scaling

Close-up view of leaf

Cluster of leaves

Tree branches

a coastline. Even your muscles grow in fractal patterns.

In the past, doctors thought of the human body as an orderly system. If the system was out of order, there was something wrong. Today, many doctors see the body as a fractal system. They know that it is natural for people to be irregular and unpredictable.

Humans aren't the only ones who grow fractally. You can see fractals almost everywhere you look in the natural world. You can see the patterns close up or far away at any scale.

When you zoom in on a single leaf, you can see fractals in the veins. When you look at a cluster of leaves, you can see fractal patterns. When you look at the way twigs branch out, you can see fractals.

in Nature

A satellite view of a forest

Oak trees

When you look at the entire tree, you can see fractals in how the branches grow. In fact, even when you look at a forest from outer space, you can see fractals.

Satellite photographs of Earth look like works of art. When the photographs are printed in color, they often resemble abstract paintings with blocks of colored shapes here and there. Rivers split as they flow. Mountains rise and fall. Coastlines move in and out.

Artists have always been inspired by nature. They have used color, light, and shadows to re-create natural textures and patterns in paintings, drawings, sculptures, and photographs. Artists also know that there are no straight lines or perfect shapes in nature.

Today, with computers and fractal programs, artists

can create landscapes in new ways. A computer fractal program can iterate many more times than an artist can with a pencil and a sheet of paper. It can also bend and twist as it iterates. This leads to quite interesting patterns! Using these patterns, artists have been able to create pictures that look like natural scenes and objects. They have also been able to create pictures of fanciful worlds and objects that are not a part of nature on Earth but look real.

You can find examples of fractal art on the Internet. There are also fractal software programs online that you can use for free or a small cost. These programs help you create your own fractal art.

"High Peaks" fractal art was created on a computer using repeated equations.

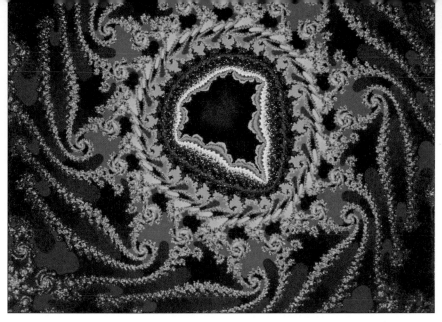
A fractal image based on the Mandelbrot Set

Geometry was created to help us describe the world in more complex ways and to build things. However, geometry has straight lines and perfect circles, and the natural world isn't made that way. Fractal geometry helps us to describe and work with the real world.

From the Stone Age to the Computer Age, the fractal patterns in nature have inspired scientists, artists, and mathematicians. We also now know that the fractals we see outside of us are patterns that exist inside of us, too. Counting the world around us began with the body. Now you can say that the art and math of fractals begin with you!

Glossary

calculation	the act or result of using arithmetic
equation	a mathematical statement that uses an equal (=) sign to show two quantities are equal
equilateral	the same or equal in length on all sides
fractal	regular or irregular shape that repeats on an increasingly smaller scale
graphic	having to do with drawing, painting, photography, or design
inspiration	something or someone that causes a bright idea or action
iterate	to repeat the same thing
random	having no specific pattern or organization
regular	formed or arranged in an ordered way
scale	a series of steps based on size or amount
shuttle	a tool used in weaving that carries a thread back and forth between threads that go up and down
symbol	an object, mark, or sign that stands for something else
taxes	money or other goods that people and businesses pay to help support a government
tessellation	shapes that fit together perfectly in a pattern